Ladybird Readers

Where Animals Live

Series Editor: Sorrel Pitts
Written by Anne Collins

LADYBIRD BOOKS

UK | USA | Canada | Ireland | Australia
India | New Zealand | South Africa

Ladybird Books is part of the Penguin Random House group of companies
whose addresses can be found at global.penguinrandomhouse.com.
www.penguin.co.uk   www.puffin.co.uk   www.ladybird.co.uk

First published by Ladybird Books, 2017
001

Text copyright © Ladybird Books Ltd, 2017

Printed in China

A CIP catalogue record for this book is available from the British Library

ISBN: 978–0–241–29868–8

All correspondence to:
Ladybird Books
Penguin Random House Children's
80 Strand, London WC2R 0RL

MIX
Paper from
responsible sources
FSC® C018179
www.fsc.org

Ladybird Readers

BBC earth

Where Animals Live

Inspired by BBC Earth TV series and
developed with input from BBC Earth
natural history specialists

Contents

Picture words

meerkats

green turtles

mountain goats

chimpanzees

hermit crabs

Arctic foxes

desert

forest

climb
(verb)

lay (eggs)
(verb)

shell

fur

flippers

hooves

7

Where animals live

Animals live in many different parts of the world. They live on hot sand, in the cold Arctic, in forests, and on mountains.

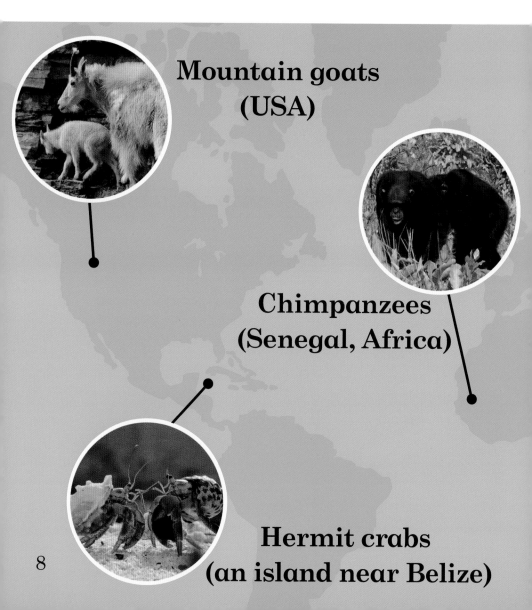

Mountain goats
(USA)

Chimpanzees
(Senegal, Africa)

Hermit crabs
(an island near Belize)

Some places are easier than others for animals to find food, stay safe, or make a home.

Animals live in all of these different places.

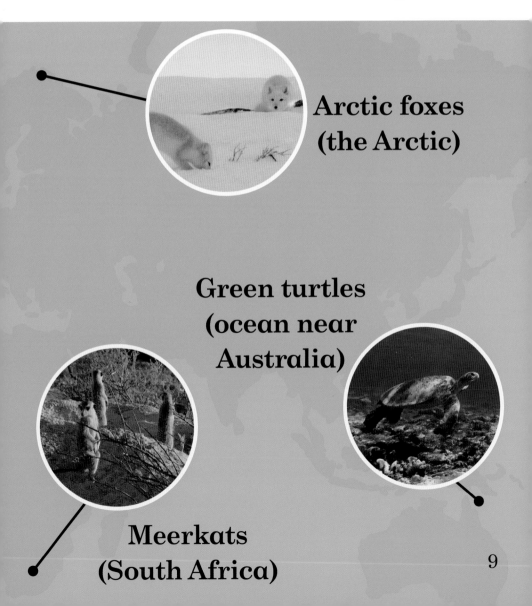

Arctic foxes (the Arctic)

Green turtles (ocean near Australia)

Meerkats (South Africa)

9

Meerkats

Meerkats live in the desert.

The desert has a lot of sand and very little water. It can get very hot, but meerkats can live well in this place.

These meerkats live in the desert in South Africa.

Meerkats have dark circles around their eyes, which help them to see in the strong sun.

Meerkats' homes

Meerkats live together with as many as 50 other meerkats.

They make their homes under the sand where it is nice and cold.

This meerkat is coming
out of its home.

13

Green turtles

Green turtles live in the ocean, in warm water.

These green turtles are swimming
in the ocean near Australia.

Turtles laying eggs

Green turtles cannot lay their eggs in the ocean.

Green turtles lay their eggs on the beach at night, when it is not hot. They use their flippers to make a place for their eggs under the sand.

shell

flipper

This green turtle
is swimming
back to the beach
to lay her eggs.

Green turtles lay many eggs
and leave them under the sand.

17

Turtles on the beach

It is difficult for green turtles
to move on the beach. Their
flippers don't work well, and
they can only move very slowly.
They can live much better in
the ocean.

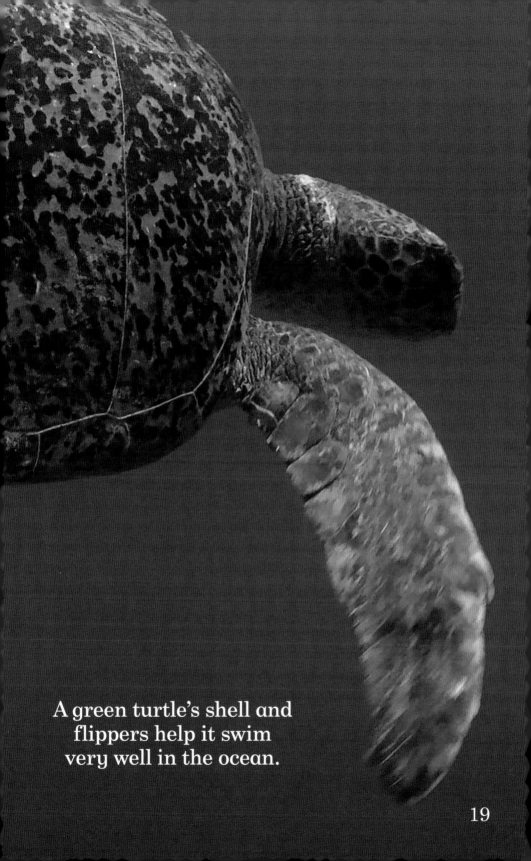

A green turtle's shell and
flippers help it swim
very well in the ocean.

Mountain goats

These mountain goats live in the mountains in the USA. They are very good at climbing and can jump nearly 3.5 meters.

These goats are climbing down the mountain.

21

Mountain climbing

Mountain goats are very safe from animals that want to catch and eat them, as no other animal can climb as well as goats! They stay in the mountains all winter.

When the weather gets warm
again, the goats climb down
the mountain to look for food.

These goats are looking
for food at the bottom
of the mountain.

Winter coats

Mountain goats have very thick coats. Their coats help them stay warm in the cold winds and snow.

thick coat

The goats are so good at climbing because of their big, strong hooves. Each hoof has two parts. This helps the goats move safely on the mountain.

hooves

Chimpanzees

These chimpanzees live together in a large family in a forest in Senegal, Africa.

When there is no rain, the forest can get very dry and hot. But when the rain comes back, the forest is green again, and there is more food and water.

This chimpanzee
lives with its family
in the forest.

Up in the trees

Chimpanzees like climbing and jumping from tree to tree. They make their nests in the trees and sleep there.

This chimpanzee
is jumping from
tree to tree.

Chimpanzees' food

The chimpanzees in this forest are very clever. They know how to get food from trees.

Chimpanzees eat fruit, plants, and other things.

The chimpanzees go to a place in the forest where there is water to drink.

The chimpanzees get in the water because it is nice and cold.

31

Hermit crabs

This is a hermit crab. It lives on an island near Belize. It carries a shell on its body. This shell is its home.

shell

The sea washes the shells on to the beach. The crabs find them and go inside them.

Many hermit crabs live on this island.

33

Safe in a shell

The island where the hermit crabs live is very hot. But the crabs are safe from the sun because of their shells.

These hermit crabs are safe inside their shells.

The shells also stop other animals and birds from eating the crabs.

A new home

When a hermit crab grows too big for its shell, it has to find a new one to live in.

There are not always enough shells on the island for each crab to have a new shell.

When a crab wants to find a new home, it sometimes has to change its shell with another crab's. The crabs make a line, and each moves out of the shell that is too small, into a bigger shell.

These crabs have made a line and are changing shells.

Arctic foxes

Arctic foxes live in the Arctic, where it is very difficult for some animals to live. It is very, very cold there.

For most of the year, there is a lot of thick snow, and it is not always easy to find food.

This Arctic fox is looking for food in the snow.

Warm fur

Arctic foxes have very thick fur and short ears, which help them to stay warm.

Their fur is white (the same as snow), so it is hard for other animals to see them. Arctic foxes have fur on the bottom of their feet, which helps them walk well on snow.

thick fur

In very cold winters, a fox can travel
95 kilometers a day to find food.

Sometimes, foxes have to
sleep on top of the snow.

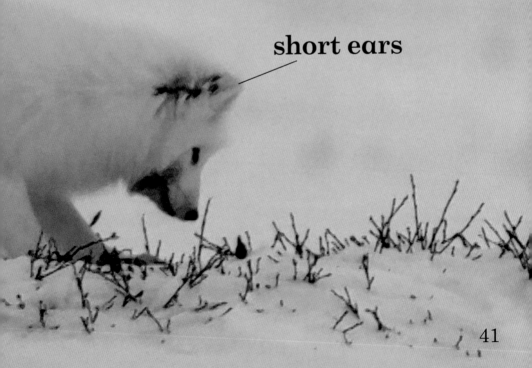

short ears

Animals' homes

All of these animals live in different places. Some places are hot, and some are very cold.

Some animals live in mountains, deserts, or forests. Others live in, or near, the sea. The animals know how to live well in their homes.

goats (high mountains)

meerkats (hot deserts)

green turtles
(warm seas)

hermit crabs
(hot beaches)

chimpanzees
(hot forests)

Arctic foxes
(cold Arctic)

Activities

The key below describes the skills practiced in each activity.

Spelling and writing

Reading

Speaking

Critical thinking

Preparation for the Cambridge Young Learners Exams

1 Match the words to the pictures.

1 meerkats

a

2 green turtle

b

3 mountain goats

c

4 chimpanzees

d

5 hermit crabs

e

6 Arctic foxes

f

2 Look and read. Put a ✓ or a ✗ in the boxes. 📖 ⭐

1 This is fur. ✓

2 These are eggs. ☐

3 These are hooves. ☐

4 This is a desert. ☐

5 This is a shell. ☐

3 Find the words.

widtb**Arctic foxes**jnvkesshellpaeforestignhdesertnbmkordmflipperstordnsihnusoiclimbrt

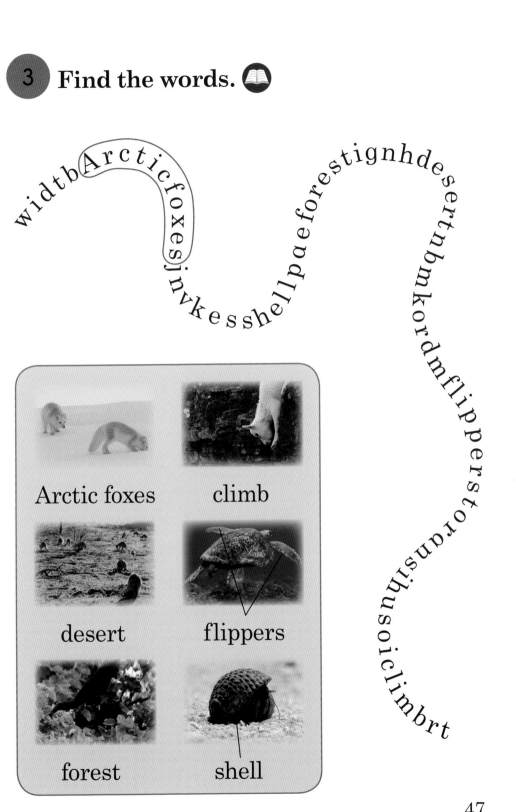

Arctic foxes

climb

desert

flippers

forest

shell

4 Choose the correct answers.

Meerkats

Meerkats live in the desert.

The desert has a lot of sand and very little water. It can get very hot, but meerkats can live well in this place.

These meerkats live in the desert in South Africa.

10

Meerkats have dark circles around their eyes, which help them to see in the strong sun.

11

Meerkats' homes

Meerkats live together with as many as 50 other meerkats.

They make their homes under the sand where it is nice and cold.

12

This meerkat is coming out of its home.

13

1 Meerkats live in the

   a desert.   **b** forest.

2 They have dark circles around their

   a eyes.   **b** mouth.

3 They . . . with other meerkats.

   a don't live   **b** live

4 They make their homes . . . the sand.

   a above   **b** under

5 They do this because it's nice and

   a cold.   **b** hot.

5 **Write the questions. Then, write the answers.** 📖 ✏️

1 (meerkats) (live) (Where) (do) (?)

Question: Where do meerkats live?

Answer: They live in the desert.

2 (flippers) (Do) (they) (have) (?)

Question:

Answer:

3 (live) (they) (?) (Do) (with) (meerkats) (other)

Question:

Answer:

6 Work with a friend. Ask and answer questions about green turtles. 🗨

Green turtles

Green turtles live in the ocean, in warm water.

These green turtles are swimming in the ocean near Australia.

Turtles laying eggs

Green turtles cannot lay their eggs in the ocean.

Green turtles lay their eggs on the beach at night, when it is not hot. They use their flippers to make a place for their eggs under the sand.

This green turtle is swimming back to the beach to lay her eggs.

shell

flipper

Green turtles lay many eggs and leave them under the sand.

1 _Which animals are these?_

They are green turtles.

2 Where do they live?

3 Where do they lay their eggs?

7 Look and read. Write *yes* or *no*.

Turtles on the beach

It is difficult for green turtles to move on the beach. Their flippers don't work well, and they can only move very slowly. They can live much better in the ocean.

A green turtle's shell and flippers help it swim very well in the ocean.

18

19

1 It is difficult for green turtles
to move on the beach. ....yes..........

2 Their flippers work well
on the beach. ....

3 They don't get hot in the sun. ....

4 They can't live well in
the ocean. ....

5 Their shells and flippers
help them swim well. ....

8 Look at the letters. Write the words.

1  e s r d t e

<u>d e s e r t</u>

2  s o r t f e

3  h e l s l

4  u r f

9 **Circle the correct pictures.**

1 This lives in the sea.

 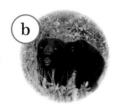 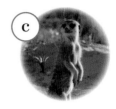

2 These have hooves.

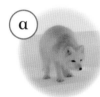  

3 These can help an animal to see well.

 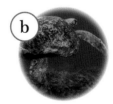 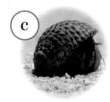

4 Chimpanzees live here.

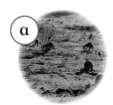  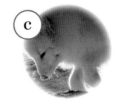

10 **Talk to your friend about these animals.** 🗨

These are mountain goats and they live in the mountains of the USA.

11 Read, and write the correct form of the verbs.

Chimpanzees

These chimpanzees live together in a large family in a forest in Senegal, Africa.

When there is no rain, the forest can get very dry and hot. But when the rain comes back, the forest is green again and there is more food and water.

This chimpanzee lives with its family in the forest.

26   27

These chimpanzees [1] ___live___ **(live)** together in a large family in a forest. When there [2] _____ **(be)** no rain, the forest can [3] _____ **(get)** very dry and hot. But when the rain [4] _____ **(come)** back, the forest is green again and there is more food and water. Chimpanzees like [5] _____ **(climb)** and jumping from tree to tree. They [6] _____ **(make)** their nests in the trees and sleep there.

12 **Ask and answer questions about the animals with a friend. Use the words in the box to help you.** 🗨 ❓

climb   walk in the snow

see in the sun   swim in the sea

jump in the trees   find shells

> *Which animals are good at climbing?*

> *Mountain goats are good at climbing.*

13 Read the text. Choose the correct words and write them on the lines.

1	above	near	under
2	on	out	up
3	into	on to	out of
4	next to	outside	inside

This is a hermit crab. It lives on an island [1] _____near_____ Belize.
It carries a shell [2] _____ its body. The shell is its home.
The sea washes the shells [3] _____ the beach. The crabs find them and go [4] _____ them.

14 Write *Why*, *Where*, *When*, or *What*.

Hermit crabs

This is a hermit crab. It lives on an island near Belize. It carries a shell on its body. This shell is its home.

shell

32

The sea washes the shells on to the beach. The crabs find them and go inside them.

Many hermit crabs live on this island. 33

1 __Where__ does this hermit crab live?
It lives on an island near Belize.

2 _____ does it carry on its body?
It carries a shell on its body.

3 _____ does it carry a shell?
Because this shell is its home.

4 _____ does a hermit crab find a new shell?
When it grows too big for its old shell.

58

15 Choose the correct words and write them on the lines. 📖 ✏️ ✨

> carry   climb   jump   lay

1 This is what green
turtles do to their eggs. _____lay_____

2 Hermit crabs do this
with shells. _____

3 Goats do this to go up
and down mountains. _____

4 Chimpanzees do this to
move from tree to tree. _____

16 Do the crossword.

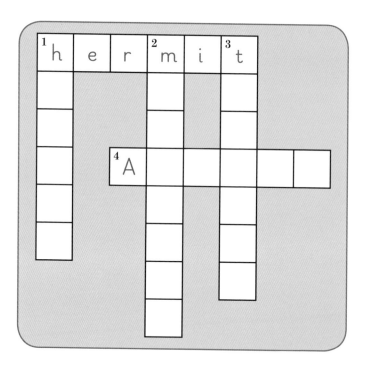

Down

1 Mountain goats have these on their feet.

2 They live in hot deserts.

3 They can be green.

Across

1 A kind of crab.

4 A kind of fox.

17 Match the two parts of the sentences.

Animals' homes

All of these animals live in different places. Some places are hot, and some are very cold.

Some animals live in mountains, deserts, or forests. Others live in, or near, the sea. The animals know how to live well in their homes.

meerkats (hot deserts)

green turtles (warm seas)

hermit crabs (hot beaches)

goats (high mountains)

chimpanzees (hot forests)

Arctic foxes (cold Arctic)

42   43

1 All of these animals

2 Some places are hot,

3 Some animals live

4 Other animals live in, or near,

5 Animals know how to

a live well in their homes.

b the sea.

c live in different places.

d in mountains, deserts, or forests.

e and some are very cold.

18 Look at the pictures. Look at the letters. Put a ✓ by the correct words.

1

a three meerkats ✓
b three meerkates ☐

2

a four chimpanzes ☐
b four chimpanzees ☐

3

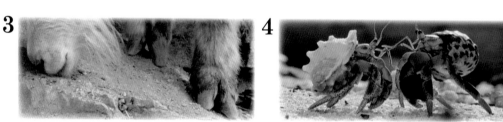

a two hoovs ☐
b two hooves ☐

4

a hermit crabs ☐
b hermit crabes ☐

5

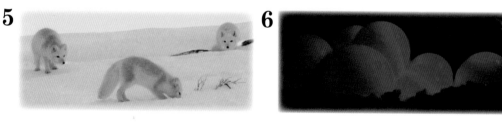

a three Arctic foxs ☐
b three Arctic foxes ☐

6

a a lot of eggs ☐
b a lot of egges ☐

19 **Circle the correct answers.**

1 Some places are . . . others for animals to find food.

(**a** easier than)

b easy than

2 No other animal can climb . . . goats!

a as good as

b as well as

3 Green turtles can live much . . . in the sea than on the beach.

a better

b gooder

4 The crabs make a line and move into . . . shells.

a more big

b bigger

Level 3

Sharks

978–0–241–25382–3

The Jungle Book

978–0–241–25383–0

The Red Knight

978–0–241–25384–7

The Elves and the Shoemaker

978–0–241–25385–4

Rapunzel

978–0–241–28394–3

Great Buildings

978–0–241–28400–1

Minibeasts

978–0–241–28404–9

Puss in Boots

978–0–241–28407–0

Jack and the Beanstalk

978–0–241–28397–4

Hansel and Gretel

978-0-241-29861-9

The Talent Show

978-0-241-29859-6

A Great Night!

978-0-241-29863-3

Bumblebee and the Rock Concert

978-0-241-29867-1

Where Animals Live

978-0-241-29868-8

Now you're ready for Level 4!